Unexpected Mentors

Unexpected Mentors

Weird & Creative Ideas
To Boost Your Career.

SHEILA MUSGROVE

I would like to graciously acknowledge all of the people I've quoted for their cleverly written words. I've made every effort to determine if their quotes were included in previously published material and required permission to reprint. If I've printed in error, please accept my apologies. Corrections will be made in future editions.

Interior design by Goran Tovilovic, www.bookclaw.com
Book cover: Lance Buckley, www.lancebuckley.com
Back cover & Chapter 12 singular photo by Kirstey Ball, www.supercorporatepeople.com
Illustrations by Bro Ojrot – Instagram: @broojrot

Join me in the conversation about "Unexpected Mentors.":
Instagram: @sheilamusgrove_author
Twitter: @SMusgrove_TAG
Facebook: @sheilamusgrove_author
LinkedIn: https://www.linkedin.com/in/sheilamusgrove/
Enroll in my blog: www.sheilamusgrove.com

ISBN Book: 978-1-9991041-0-8

ISBN eBook: 978-1-9991041-1-5

For Mom-Betty

What the heck does a *rubber duck* have to do with unexpected mentors?

Keep reading and you'll find out!

Chapter Index

Introduction:

The first time I was asked to do a keynote on my mentors... my initial reaction was,

...well, shoot, I've never had a formal mentor, *so what the heck will I talk about???*

I laughed out loud when this image popped into my mind.
Peter Lehman's *Mentor* red wine. HA.

I could certainly talk for an hour about the virtues of a good, solid red wine and how it helped shape my career! GRIN.

This little book started as a 50-minute keynote address at a "Backpacks to Briefcases" event for the business students at a Canadian college. Later that year, I was asked to deliver the convocation address for the same college. They said,

"Hey, we loved your keynote from earlier in the year...could you do a *rapid-fire* version for our graduates?"

They gave me 8 minutes.

Seriously? I can hardly say hello in 8 minutes, so it was a BIG challenge! ☺

My goal was to be memorable.

I wanted each student to remember at least one nugget from my address.

We've all sat through numerous graduation speeches. And, well, the convocation speaker is usually DULLLLLLLLLLLLLLLLL.

I. Did. Not. Want. To. Be. DULL. HA.

I did it.

It was sharp.

Witty.

People laughed.

It was memorable.

Nailed it.

The feedback from parents and students was amazing!

> "We went to a get-together tonight with several of my daughter's graduate friends....and **hands down your speech MADE a huge impact on all of them**. In Courtney's words, yours was the best and most meaningful message they heard today."

> Tracey W. Red Deer, Alberta, Canada

> I attended my daughter's RDC convocation ceremony. I wanted to drop you a quick message and let you know I enjoyed your speech. **It was inspirational and entertaining!** I remembered just about everything you talked about! I am sure everyone appreciated your message."

> Miranda C. Red Deer, Alberta, Canada

Over the past few years I've continued to edit-expand-evolve a version of the *Unexpected Mentors* speech that has been a hit with audiences of every size and career level, across Canada.

But the tipping point when I decided to turn it into a book?

I was asked to deliver a dinner keynote for a business women's conference in beautiful Jasper, Alberta.

I was thrilled to be invited.

I grew up in the little town beside Jasper. It was a great trip down memory lane to be back in my old home town.

My mom, Betty, was in the audience (and there to hug everyone in the room after my talk).

Sidebar: I tell stories about Mom in my newsletter (more on that later). She is mentioned in my keynotes. She's always at my client parties. Everyone knows her as "Mom-Betty".

The conference organizers hosted a lovely buffet dinner.

Loads of choices.

And a dessert table that went on forever.

Wine was flowing.

The room was warm.

So, an audience with full tummies. A bit of wine. And, heat...

Uh oh. That's a recipe for a nap and drowsy eyes.

When I hit the stage, I knew I had to **BRING IT**.

I had to keep them leaning in and on the edge of their seat.

Boom! The organizer had the BEST feedback ever...

"Sheila, that was f'ing FABULOUS."

And, in *THAT* moment, this book was born.

The traditional idea of a mentor and mentee is a formal relationship.

Quite honestly, I've always thought it was all a bit stuffy.

You put your trust in ONE person to guide your career.

Sounds pretty risky to me.

So, I've really never liked the idea of a formal mentor.

I like the inspiration and guidance that comes from a potpourri of unexpected people, things, moments and experiences. Both good and not so good.

Mentors also come from experiences that are not career highlights. Even huge flops. Yes, it's true. I'll share some of mine.

The idea of an *Unexpected Mentor* puts you in the driver's seat of where you want to take your career *at any stage* and where you can find oodles of career inspiration.

Yes, *oodles*. GRIN.

You'll learn some unexpected, weird and creative ideas of where you can find inspiration and mentorship for your career. Chances are, you've overlooked, under-valued or never thought of most of these career boosters as unexpected mentors.

I know. It's a crazy idea. You need to look at the idea of mentors with fresh eyes.

"If you are not willing to risk the unusual, you will have to settle for the ordinary."

Jim Rohn, author

Why would you ever want to leave something as HUGE as your career success in the hands of *anyone other than yourself?*

You have resources you've never tapped.

You'll learn *how to be your own mentor.*

Let's dive in.

Unexpected Mentor 1:

People Closest To You

My parents were the strongest mentors in shaping the core of who I am. They were my first mentors of what it takes to be a successful entrepreneur.

They taught me work ethic and what it means to show up ready to work each day and what it means to work hard.

Mom and Dad both worked day jobs. From the time I was 6, they also had side businesses on the go.

Dad was my first sales mentor.

Years ago, there was a home-based business that was well ahead of its time with environmentally friendly, biodegradable household cleaning and natural health products.

Part of the business presentation was a product demo which (from my little kid vantage point) was a bit like a magic show.

Our living room would be filled with people and Dad stood in the middle leading the demonstrations. He was quite the story teller and loved doing these demos.

His favourite demo was a product that took rust or discolouration out of white laundry. He'd take a glass of water – squirt some red dye into the glass and *tell the story about when he did a load of laundry and accidentally put a red sock in with the whites.*

Everyone GASPED…

…as they visualized a dreadful load of pink laundry. OMG.

He'd slowly add some of the special powder to the red water, give it a stir and *Voila! The water turned clear and he'd be grinning from the inside out.*

After he'd hook everyone with the product demo, he went to the white board (yes, I grew up with a white board in my living room) and drew the business opportunity.

I remember sitting close by and listening to the presentation and seeing how engaging he was.

Of course, 6-year old me didn't realize I was being given an incredible lesson on how to be a natural sales person and a great story teller.

My parents built a successful business over many years.

In fact, they had a mini convention for their team and I got to do a keynote! I think I was 15 or 16. I was thrilled to be at the podium sharing what a great learning experience it was to watch Mom and Dad grow their business.

The imprint of entrepreneurship, sales and business from my parents made an enormous impact on me.

I recall the very young me seeing a business magazine with a woman on the cover. She was wearing a navy suit and carrying a navy briefcase.

I *knew* that would be me.

And, somehow that image was hardwired into my little kid brain and never left.

The only thing that changed was I now wear black suits and carry a red briefcase!

My parents taught me the hardwiring of entrepreneurship, creativity and values from a very young age.

I'm sure you've had people like this in your life too. If you think back, your family and close friends and those who you look up to, have mentored you through many life experiences.

**Mentor
Moment**

Your Turn!

Throughout the chapters, you'll see this *mentor moment* image. It's a signal for you to do an *unexpected mentor* big brain thinking exercise.

Have fun with being creative (and maybe a bit crazy off-the-charts) with each *mentor moment* exercise!

Think about who influenced your career hard wiring. Who has influenced your:

- Communication style
- Leadership skills
- Problem solving
- Humour
- Work ethic
- Business sense
- Sales abilities
- Resilience
- Team work
- Compassion

Think about your parents, spouse, aunts, uncles, cousins, family friends, neighbours, coaches, teachers...*you get the drift!*

Who are your unexpected mentors?

What have they taught you already?

What are they continuing to teach you?

Unexpected Mentor 2:

Crappy Career Moments

Throughout grade school and high school I was an OK student – at best a B student. It's fun to look back at school and think *how the heck did I ever make it out OK??*

I was part of the band... *another way of saying I wasn't part of the hip crowd. GRIN.*

I was like the Simpsons character, Lisa Simpson, and I played the saxophone.

Who knew Lisa and I share the love of saxophones AND crazy sticky-up hair?

Our band was doing extra rehearsals in preparation for a big concert. One very early practice, my band teacher leaned down and said to me,

"Sheila, you actually have *zero* rhythm."

I did actually laugh as he was right.   Even though he was an ass for saying so!

He became a mentor who showed me I *wasn't going* to be a professional musician!

I was able to laugh as my parents had taught me that I wasn't going to win every time or be good at every single thing I try. And, while my feelings might have been hurt a little, I knew he was right.

Here's one of my biggest crappy career moments.

I had a brief stint at a telecom company early in my career. I thought it was going to be my long-term career company. The head office was local. They were on a huge growth trajectory. (I thought my career would be too!)

I joined a brand-new division. Gorgeous office. Beautiful furniture. Not an expense was spared. Imported stone tiles. Top of the line everything. Cutting edge technology too.

I was excited for my new career. It was a third-party call centre.

My role was to design the key metrics and deliverables for each client and communicate results, action plans and such.

I felt pretty comfortable in my role within a few months.

I was in a weekly meeting with a key client. Conversation was good. Results of his campaign were solid. Everything was on-track.

Until....

My Operations Vice President barged into the meeting.

He inappropriately said,

"What the f*ck is going on?
Why are you meeting with him?"

Without another word, he abruptly turned and walked out of the meeting room, with a big Cheshire cat grin on his face. He was pleased with his outburst for whatever bizarre reason.

I was beyond embarrassed with his extremely unprofessional outburst.

So was my client!

My VP's comments were unprofessional and random.

My job was to meet with clients to ensure they were happy with their campaigns.

His outburst made ZERO sense.

I apologized to my client and quickly wrapped up our meeting.

I walked into my VP's office and said,

"You are a Vice President.
That was not the behavior of a Vice President.
Do not ever swear at me or speak to me in that tone again."

I was shaking. Mad. Embarrassed. Humiliated.

I wanted to run out of the office and never return.

It was a *CRAPPY* career moment.

The news of his outburst spread as fast as my bold rebuttal.

The Sales VP asked the president if I could move to his department. I delightedly moved to his team.

The crazy Operations VP? Well, let's just say his career took a dive and he wasn't in a VP role for much longer.

There were many lessons in this *crappy career moment*, with the obvious being how to never speak to an employee or client. I'm sure the Operations VP knew his actions were inappropriate, but he did it anyway. As much as I had career aspirations of achieving a VP title, I knew I'd NEVER act like he did that day.

Mentor Moment

Your Turn!

Dig deep. Think about some of your moments that didn't go so well.

Yes, at the time they were crappy, just as mine was.

What did the crappy moment teach you about what you wanted in your career?

How has that crappy moment shaped your career?

Unexpected Mentor 3:
Big Mistakes & Kicks In The Pants

I confess. I needed a kick in the pants. I was stalled on an e-book version of my book.

Here's the story:

It wasn't until the first few hundred copies of my first book arrived that I realized something BIG was missing.

My heart sank.

I lived and breathed that book for months. It went through countless drafts.

How did I miss such a big error?

And, here it was....

The table of contents was missed. Yes, the ENTIRE chapter outline.

Imagine how challenging it would be to read the e-book version of the book without a table of contents?

Sooooo, it sat on my to do list for months.

Here comes the kick in the pants.

I was out with a friend for dinner. Great conversation. Lots of laughter.

He simply asked, "Why haven't you released an e-book version?"

I quickly explained my missing table of contents debacle.

His reply,

" Well, darling, I can't imagine adding it would be that difficult. After all, you've already written an <u>entire</u> book, so you could likely figure out how to add the table of contents. "

I'm fairly certain there was a wee smug look on his face at that moment when he knew I'd just been dragging my heels AND I had absolutely no good come-back.

Well, the kick in the pants worked. He was right. It wasn't hard to add the table of contents.

And, I'm thrilled to report the e-book version is available worldwide. 🙂

A swift kick
in the pants
$1.00

Mistakes can stall a project. The "to do" to fix the mistake often seems gigantic. So, you procrastinate.

Once you get out of your head and down to work…. it's likely easy to fix.

Maybe you need a kick in the pants even though you haven't made a mistake. It can also just be *you're stalling to get started*.

**Mentor
Moment**

Your Turn!

Where do you need a kick in the pants so you keep moving forward?

What projects have taken a permanent place on your to do list?

Set aside 30 minutes to work on your stalled "to do" item. I bet you'll surprise yourself on how much you can accomplish. I know I did!

Tuck this little *"kick in the pants"* question in the back of your mind. Believe me, you'll need a kick in the pants *MANY* times in your career.

I know I have!

"My best successes came on the heels of failures."

Barbara Corcoran,
real estate mogul & TV personality

Unexpected Mentor 4:

Books Are *BIG* Mentors

Since opening my company, my biggest mentors have been leading thought authors. They were my best companions in helping me shape what my company looks like today.   (And they also don't cost much!)

Anytime I'm stumped about a business issue – I know the answers are on my bookshelves at home.

This is my weird collection of books and inspiration.

Many things are on my shelves for nostalgia and fun. Old school encyclopedias – I loved them as a kid. A disco ball. A leopard print hat (why not?) Yes, sometimes I wear it while reading!

My top 4 author mentors are:

1. **Seth Godin** – he is considered to be the world's best marketer. His writing fueled and energized the creative side of branding and marketing for my company.

His first book, *"Purple Cow"* stuck with me. He shares a story of driving through France with his family and seeing hundreds of brown cows. He thought – *wouldn't it be interesting if one of those cows was purple*. He said "now *that* would be remarkable."

He defines being remarkable as being worthy of remarking about.

I actually met Seth years ago. He simply signed my *Purple Cow* book, "Moo."

I took a chance and showed him my business card. I asked, "What do you think?"

After a moment, he said, "This is the second-best business card I've ever seen." From the world's best marketer, I'll take second. GRIN.

Here's what the world's second-best business card looks like!

Yes, that's a hole in the bottom circle.

People touch it. They stick their pens in it and twirl the card. They remember it. (And, because of the hole, we tend to win more business card draws. GRIN.)

2. **Tony Hseith – Founder of Zappos & Author of *Delivering Happiness*.** Zappos is an online shoe company. I can say I'm very happy when snazzy shoes get delivered to my office!

Tony talks about culture as being a critical part of your brand. After reading his book, a disco ball was installed in our office kitchen, the gong was ordered for our reception area and our office play list broke all rules with the addition of ACDC, Calvin Harris, Flo Rida and the like!

When candidates enter the TAG office, they always remark on the music vibe...a little hard rock adds to the ambience!

3. **Napoleon Hill –** *Think and Grow Rich.* This book is ancient but contains some absolute gems. I re-read this book once a year. I "borrowed" my copy from my parents' bookshelf years ago. It's tattered. A bit wrinkled. The pages are yellow. *It's my most treasured book.*

It gives me new ideas and different perspectives each time I read it. It also reinforces many principles that help me continue to strive for success in my career.

4. **Canadian author, Michael Losier** wrote an amazing little best-selling book called the *Law of Attraction.* I learned the power of intention and the power of words to attract what you want into your life.   It was positive stuff to put into my head to shape success thoughts early on.

Yes, there are words that work better than others. This is a book that should be on your bookshelf. I've read this book so many times, I can almost repeat it verbatim!

"A book is a dream you hold in your hands."

Nat Carson, photographer

**Mentor
Moment**

Your Turn!
What books have influenced you?

What books are on your "must-read" list?

Need some inspiration? Here's a great list of "must-read" books:

https://www.goodreads.com/list/show/10571.The_100_Best_Business_Books_of_All_Time

(I love Dr. Seuss is on the list!)

"Always read something that will make you look good if you die in the middle of it."

P.J. O'Rourke, political satirist & journalist

Unexpected Mentor 5:

Far-Fetched Ideas

From the time I could read, my first career ambition was to be a writer.

I love books of all genres.

Goofy little kid books.

Serious history books.

Business books.

Sappy love stories.

Classics.

One of my treasured childhood books still makes me smile:

"Otherwise Known As Sheila The Great.",
by Judy Bloom.

Prior to seeing this book, I thought Sheila was a weird name. I wanted to change my name to Wanda. (I recently shared this tid-bit with Mom-Betty. We both chuckled.)

After seeing my weird name on the cover of Judy Bloom's book, I was OK to remain Sheila.

These childhood authors inspired me to think that one day I could write a book too.

And it was a dream that never left me.

I'll be honest.

Writing a book seemed like *a really big far-fetched idea.*

Yes, far-fetched.

We all have far-fetched ideas that are branded into our brains.

Some ideas have been there since we first started dreaming as a little kid. Others pop up throughout your career.

Regardless of how long they've been etched into your brain, they sit in the back of our minds and simmer. Far-fetched ideas are just like a good home-made tomato sauce. It needs simmering time (and a little red wine for flavour. GRIN.)

After some time, if you let them, those far-fetched ideas become a bit more realistic. They are still crazy (and lofty), yet *somewhat* doable.

After a good amount of simmer time, the idea becomes *far-stretched.*

What's far-stretched?

Far-stretched to me is a crazy-ass goal that might just sprout legs and become real. It's still a lofty idea...but, it might happen.

My *far-stretched* idea was
to write a book.

I recall a writing lesson in grade 4. It was something to do with trees. I was struggling and Mom came to the rescue.

OK. I'll be honest. She wrote most of it.

Mom and I still giggle that my teacher LOVED what she wrote and wasn't so fond of what I had written.

I remember reading and re-reading what she wrote. It was really good. It became hardwired into my grade 4 brain on how to write compelling stories. Even about trees. HA.

Mom is very creative. She loves writing letters. When she was younger, she'd write letters to her mom and sisters. I always loved reading what she'd written. She'd tell stories and updates on our family's activities. And, she'd light up when there was a reply letter from her mom or sisters. I loved reading those letters too!

When we travel, she brings notepaper to capture the days events and sights taken in. I love reading how she views our adventures!

From stories about trees to years and years of letter writing and story-telling, my mom was my first writing mentor.

(Mom-Betty in action!)

**Mentor
Moment**

Your Turn!

What are some of your far-fetched AND far-stretched ideas?

What's close to moving into the far-stretched category? *If not, what would it take for your far-fetched ideas to become far-stretched....and kind of doable??*

And, yes, far-stretched ideas usually *scare the s!!#$@%* out of us! GRIN.

Unexpected Mentor 6:

Moments Can Be Mentors

I heard an amazing speaker who gave me a *"mentor moment"*.

He encouraged us to stretch to make daring *asks* in our daily lives.

Be Bold and Just Ask was his message.

I took it to heart. If you ask for crazy things, you do hear the word NO. But eventually you hear the word YES more often!

Ask if you can meet the lead singer after a concert. Ask your boss if you can take their snazzy new car for a spin. Ask if you can take the empty front row seats at a game. Ask for an appointment with a CEO you'd NEVER expect to get a yes from.

You're on track when you ask for stuff and you expect to get a big NO.

If you ask enough, eventually you get a YES. And, some pretty cool experiences. But you have to be bold and just ask.

The idea resonated with me and has never left.

I had just started writing my first book, "Hired!". I was headed to work and listening to the radio.

These two cool cats were being interviewed. Jason and Aly are known as **The Style Guys**. They are on virtually every Canadian red carpet as they are experts on fashion.

I thought,
wouldn't it be cool to quote "THE STYLE GUYS" in my Dressing Sharp chapter?

OMG. I couldn't wait to get to the office and reach them before I lost my nerve.

I found their website and sent them an email.

And, wouldn't you know it...they said YES!

They gave some terrific insight for the *Dressing Sharp* chapter. And, they even gave me permission to use their super-cool photo in my book!

I was stoked.

With a big cheesy grin
on my face, I thought,

"Who else could I
be bold and just ask"?

I reached this handsome cool cat from TSN. His name is Cory Woron and he's an anchor on TSN's golf channel.

My ask to Cory was,

"What do you do to prepare to go on live television and interview someone like Tiger Woods?"

The prep to go on live television is similar to the level of nerves and preparation to go into a job interview. I thought it would be great material for my interview chapter.

And, to my surprise, he said yes! And, he gave me a golden interview! He spoke about his set falling on his head and having to go on live television slightly concussed. (He was ok.)

Pressing my luck a bit further, I asked TSN for permission to use his official headshot. GRIN. They said yes!

BE BOLD. Just Ask.

I was on a roll and reached out to Tim Tamashiro. He's the former CBC radio host of *Jazz Tonic*, recording artist and best-selling author. I asked Tim the same thing.

"What do you do to prepare to go on stage?"

Tim shared he imagines smelling Crayola wax crayons before going on stage. (What???? HA.)

He read an article suggesting simply imagining the smell of wax crayons will bring your blood pressure down. GRIN. It might be worth giving it a whirl!

I was having a BALL being bold and just asking!

I continued to ask senior executives and presidents of companies to be quoted in my book.

I asked them to share their favourite interview questions; what they'd love to see more from candidates and the best end of interview question they've been asked.

Sidebar – I was writing my book in the height of a *very deep recession*. Loads of lay-offs and downsizing. It certainly wasn't a time when anyone was interested in having a chat with a recruiter.

But by asking for their advice, I met senior executives who otherwise would NOT have met with a recruiter.

Many people I asked were open to being interviewed by a newbie-aspiring author.

And, honestly, it became a great sales and networking tool. I was able to reach out to countless executives to say,

"Hey, we don't know each other, but I'm writing a book...can I quote you?"

Loads of people didn't even reply. But, 14 did.
I ended up with golden material from their wisdom and insights.

A weird thing happens when you write a book.

It gives you permission to be **BOLD.**

OK, I'll say it...

A$$-clenching BOLD.

Want to know my first a$$-clenching move??

I sent copies of the book to the Prime Minister of Canada and his wife.

I signed the books and sent along a formal letter.

My ASK to the Prime Minister:

How can we get "HIRED!" into the hands of 1.4 million Canadians who are searching for employment?

Political preferences aside….

Wouldn't it be cool if they came back with an order for 1.4 million books??

Kind of a big-ass long shot! *You just never know unless you ask.*

My heart skipped a beat when I saw the gold embossed envelope from 24 Sussex (the official residence of the Prime Minister of Canada).

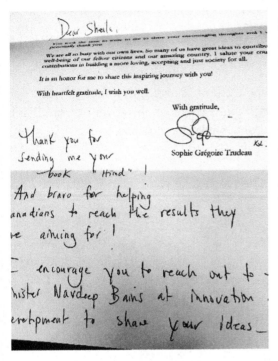

The letter was from Sophie Trudeau. (The Prime Minister's wife.) I was THRILLED to receive a response.

The really special part was her handwritten note...complete with the two xx's on her signature!

She took time to personalize the letter.

I was touched and impressed.

Sure, I would've been OVER THE FREAKING MOON if she sent a letter AND an order for 1.4 million copies of my book!

Two years after my book was published, I'm still being BOLD and Just Asking.

My most recent crazy bold idea...I'm determined to get my book into Hallmark for graduation season. I sent a copy of my book along with a letter to the Procurement department in Canada and their USA headquarters.

I had the letter translated into Dutch and sent off copies to their European headquarters.

And, for fun, I just sent a copy of my book to Ellen Degeneres. Imagine how many of her viewers need solid resume and interviewing advice?

I recently wrote a letter to the CEO of Guess. I'm wearing these fabulous shiny, red steel toed guess shoes on the cover of "Hired!". I have them in black, gold, bone, snakeskin and red.

You get the idea. I **LOVE** these shoes!

But they are discontinued.

My ask to the CEO of Guess is to help keep me in supply of these discontinued shoes. And, from every stage I stand on – I'll give a shout out to Guess. Stay tuned. You never know what will happen!

I dare you...

Be A$$-clenching BOLD and JUST ASK.

Mentor Moment

Your Turn!

What are your Be A$$-clenching BOLD & JUST ASK Ideas? *Be creative and crazy with what you could ask for!*

What's your deadline? *Which ones will you do today? Tomorrow? This week?*

I double-dare you.

BE A$$-CLENCHING BOLD & JUST ASK. Go THERE.

"It's better to be absolutely ridiculous than absolutely boring."

Marilyn Munro, actress

Unexpected Mentor 7

The Pick-Your-Brain Coffee Meeting Is A Bad Idea

Your head is likely spinning after writing down your *a$$-clenching, be bold and just ask* ideas. Before you run off with your list of BOLD ideas...

A few WARNINGS.

I know secretly you've been thinking about who you can call to get some career ideas. You'd love a personal mini-mentor session. You'd like to book an hour or so with someone you look up to professionally to get some career nuggets.

That's ok. But consider you're asking for their professional expertise and their time on an already extremely busy schedule. Know their to-do list goes on for pages.

Here's my experience.

I get calls and emails daily asking if I'd be able to take a "quick" look at someone's resume and give some feedback.

What they're really asking for is a free professional assessment.

I always ask the question,

"Have you read my book, "*Hired!*"?

If they have, I'm pleased to take a look at their resume and I'll email some feedback, if I'm not buried on a big project.

(Hint: Email during business hours, not at 3AM when SPAM email comes in, as I'll likely accidentally delete. And, use a subject line other than "resume". As a recruiter, I probably receive a hundred or so resumes each day with that exact same subject line. GRIN.)

One job seeker said they'd read it. I opened the resume and replied a split second later with,

"Please re-read the entire chapter on resumes."

If you're asking a professional for their opinion, you need to do your homework. Research their blogs, books, podcasts, and videos. Don't expect them to give you a front row seat to a live and in person synopsis of their expertise. *(Yes, that was meant to poke you a bit. You need to ensure you've put some effort in.)*

Here's the #1 thing NOT to do
(everyone does it, but you won't.)

Do not approach the mini-mentor with this goofy question:

"Hey, can I *pick your brain?*"

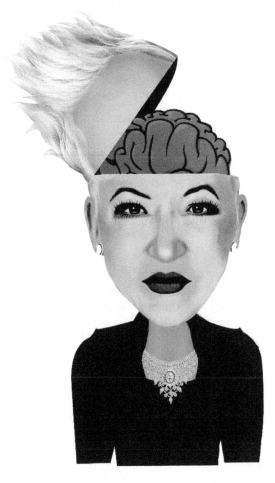

The image that pops to mind, is someone literally picking at my brain. HA.

Or, even weirder, I envision a documentary about monkeys in the wild, picking bugs off each other. Ewwwwwwww.

You get it. Neither image is good.

What you're really asking for is for someone to set aside time to provide free coaching advice by parting with 15, 30 **or 60 minutes of their time.**

Most people offer to buy their unexpected mentor a cup of coffee.

Psssst. A latte isn't a big draw for most busy professionals.

You need to approach it differently.

Here's 9 tips on how to secure a mini-mentor phone meeting or email exchange:

1. **Don't go in cold.** If you've never met the person, chances are your call or email won't even get a reply.

2. **Connect through LinkedIn** – find some common ground. Do you know common connections? Did you attend the same school? Same degree? Charities in common? Always add a personal note to your LinkedIn connection request on your common thread.

3. **Do NOT ask for the coffee meeting in the initial connection request.** *(It's like dating – you can't ask someone out the minute you match on a dating app. You need to connect, have a chat and figure out if you'd like to meet. GRIN.)*

4. **Be careful with:** *"I know "so and so".* She suggested I reach you for some advice."* I still don't know you. Which leads me to....

5. **Be specific on what you want help with.** I always give time to people who call or email and say, "I'm looking to publish my first book. Might you have 15 minutes for a phone call to talk about how you've marketed *"Hired*"? It's specific. Chances are, I can spare 10 – 15 minutes for a phone call. Maybe not today, but probably in the near future. They've been specific on the question they'd like to talk about (and I can realistically cover in a brief conversation).

6. If you ask for a **phone meeting,** versus meeting for coffee or lunch, you'll have a much higher chance of the conversation taking place. An in person meeting always takes more time. Go for the phone call. *Note: If you can't secure a phone call – shift gears and ask if you can send them a few short questions by email instead.*

7. **Know that you're asking for time and expertise** – the busy professional won't likely get a return on their time investment with you. It's funny, when people ask for the *"pick-your-brain coffee meeting"*, most truly think it's flattering for the professional. And, sure they've got lots to share, but chances of them getting a pay-back on their time investment is low.

8. **Be prepared. Be on time for the call. Don't push your luck and ask too many questions. Acknowledge when the time is up.**

9. **Follow up with a thank you note or email.** Good manners are always in fashion. And, who knows, you may get a second opportunity for another insightful 15-minute conversation in the future!

**Mentor
Moment**

Your Turn!

What specific information are you looking for from the mini-mentor conversation? *(Write out your top questions, ensuring they're targeted. The question, "What's the best career advice you could give?", isn't targeted. It's lazy. Be specific.)*

Who would you like to have a mini-mentor phone conversation with? Why? *(Have you explored their blogs, books, podcasts and videos? Do your homework.)*

Just say no to *"brain-picking"*.

Unexpected Mentor 8:

Paid Mentors & Do Things That Scare The Sh!t Out Of You

Yes, those things.

It's easy to say NO to those crazy ideas floating around in your head. We've all talked ourselves out of them and then later regretted it.

I had a goal of writing a book since I was in grade two. It was hard-wired into my little kid brain and it wasn't budging.

Over the last decade (or longer) I'd go through writing bursts. I'd write like mad. And after those bursts, I wouldn't like a thing I'd written, so it would get buried somewhere on my laptop not to be seen for months or even years.

I'll be honest with you. Writing a book is scary. I put myself out there for criticism. It could get bad reviews. It didn't matter. I HAD to write it.

In August of 2015, *I gave myself a kick in the ass* and said,

Let's get this done.

That's when I hired an expert editor.

For the next 4 months, I parked my butt in my home office each weekend and wrote. I had a deadline and a goal. To keep on track, I had chapters due to Kim, my editor, each Monday.

Sometimes you have to be willing to invest in yourself with a paid mentor or expert. She guided me through the gargantuan task of writing a book.

I'm often asked, "Why has "HIRED!" been so successful?"

It's because it doesn't read like a text book...or any other resume book out there. Thank goodness!

It's written in a tone that sounds like the reader and I are having a conversation.

When I started the writing process, I sent Kim my first 2 chapters that I'd written years ago.

I was soooooo excited for her feedback!

Two days later we were on our scheduled call and she said,

"Who the hell wrote this shit? Oh wait, before you answer, let me take the fork out of my eye!"

She said, "Sheila - I've known you for a decade. You are fun and a stand out. *This isn't fun.*"

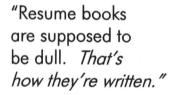

My shaky reply?

"Resume books are supposed to be dull. *That's how they're written.*"

My expert editor didn't miss a beat,

"Why would you want to write another book just like every other dull resume book on the market?"

Hmmmm. Good point. *That's why you hire an expert.* GRIN.

So, thankfully she coaxed my fun writing voice out! Otherwise, my book would be just as dull and boring as all of the other books in the genre.

Hiring Kim as a formal writing mentor was a critical decision – she gave me a blueprint to follow to accomplish the massive goal of writing a book. And, thank goodness, she convinced me to write with personality!!

At some point in your career, paying an expert mentor can be worth its weight in gold!

It sure was for me.

Rewind to March 2016 when my book launched.

I had no idea my world was about to turn upside down (in a good way).

"Hired!" hit the Amazon best-seller lists in both Canada and the USA within 24 hours of going live.

It debuted at #31 in the USA and #2 in Canada.

I giggled with Mom that night – I was exhausted after all of the excitement. **So, if I'd envisioned what my night would be like after becoming a best-selling author,** I'd have thought champagne, a glamorous dinner out, flashing lights....

Well, I was in my house with a tofurky wrap, a blanket, my cat Phoebe and Netflix...and a glass or two of wine.   Yes, it's true.

Not at all the glitz and glamour I would have expected. And seriously? No paparazzi? Not one, I assure you.

Within 6 days we were #1 in Canada.

I wrote and sent a formal press release with the exciting news.

A well-known Canadian national book retailer, Indigo Chapters, picked up my press release and called to request a meeting. GASP.

When you're a newbie author and Indigo Chapters calls you...you drop what you're doing and get your butt to that meeting as fast as your stilettos will take you.

In that meeting, *their ask* was my permission to put my book into their online store! Ummmmm, yes! As a result, my book is also available in select stores in Calgary, Vancouver, Red Deer and Ottawa. It has also brought me many media interviews right across Canada.

To say I was *over the moon* is an understatement!

Do you have career goals that scare the SH!T out of you?

Pssst. *If your career goals don't scare the sh!t out of you, they're likely not lofty enough.*

To reach those lofty, off the charts career goals, at some point in your career you should consider hiring a paid mentor or expert.

It can be a game changer. It sure was for me.

**Mentor
Moment**

Your Turn!

What are the crazy bold ideas you've got floating around in your head? *Yes, the ones that you keep saying NO to, because they scare the sh!t out of you!*

Where could you use expert mentorship in your career? Who do you know?

Who is your dream mentor?

If paying for a mentor seems out of reach – don't chicken out.
What skills can you offer in exchange?

Sidebar: It's a wonder I've been able to write any sentences, let alone two books, with my attentive giant cat Phoebe. She likes to rest on my keyboard and keep a close eye on what I'm writing. *She's my unpaid mentor!* GRIN.

Education Is An Endless Springboard

Your education WAS just a SPRINGBOARD.

It's taught you far more than your classes.   It's NOT the finish line. It doesn't define (or limit) where you take your career next.

You might get a chuckle out of my educational path.

My clerk typist certificate is from a small educational consortium in northern Alberta.

My diploma from Red Deer College is from the legal assistant program.

My degree is in law in the liberal arts with a minor in Soviet East European studies. *Seriously, that still makes me chuckle.*

What on earth was I thinking I'd ever do with that degree??

As an entrepreneur, recruiter, author and speaker – one would have assumed my education ***should have been in***: English, Business, Entrepreneurial studies or HR. It clearly wasn't.

My education taught me how to write, how to position an argument and how to balance a full course load while working and going to school.

In short, it taught me how to work super hard. **And, how to use that knowledge in completely unrelated career choices.**

You get to decide the many amazing and creative ways to use your education.

No matter what point you're at in your career or how many years ago you were in school.

And, that's straight from a legal assistant, law in the liberal arts with a minor in Soviet East European studies degree holder...who decided to launch a recruitment firm and write a best-selling book. (GRIN)

Mentor Moment

Your Turn!

Outside of the OBVIOUS, what did you *really* learn from your education?

How can you use your education to guide the next step in your career?

Unexpected Mentor 10:
You're Not Too "Whatever"

This chapter is short but sweet and you need it.

WHATEVER

No, you're not *too old*, *too young*, *too whatever* to take your career in a different direction.

I launched my recruitment firm and became an entrepreneur at 38.

I published my first book 2 months before my 50th birthday. I started to speak regularly as part of my business only *after* my book was published.

In essence, I started a new, high-profile career at 50.

So, NO, you're not too old.

Too young.

Too whatever.

Mentor Moment

Your Turn!

What would you like to do for a career, but you have crushed the idea because you think...

I'm too old, too young or too "whatever"?

What's your *"whatever"* ?

"Without leaps of imagination, or dreaming, we lose the excitement of possibilities. Dreaming after all, is a form of planning."

Gloria Steinem,
feminist, journalist, and social political activist

Unexpected Mentor 11:

Your Inner Kid RUNS The Show

This is me - about the time I was cooking up the idea of being an author.

This picture makes me chuckle.

I'm in grade 2.

No front teeth. Lopsided pigtails. Freckles.

My grandmother made this outfit. Red hot pants (that's really what they were called)

(And, I know you've just remembered your own funny grade 2 picture!)

This picture sits on my home office desk.

Two reasons.

1. Honestly, I can't ever take myself too seriously when she's staring back at me.

2. It reminds me to keep listening to my inner kid.

Listen to the inner little kid in your head who holds onto those crazy goals of what you really wanted to be when you grew up.

Little kids know exactly what they like and they're absolutely clear on what they don't like. (And, usually broccoli comes up on that list. HA.)

They are creative. Everything seems possible. They are dreamers and inspired by cartoon characters, story books and whatever their little kid eyes see next.

My little kid wasn't letting go of me being in business nor was she letting me not write a book.

Sometimes she's been a real pain in the ass but I love her.

"May you always have a beginner's mind."

Japanese Proverb

**Mentor
Moment**

Your Turn!

As we start to grow up, sometimes our lofty crazy-kid ideas get stuffed away because they don't seem realistic.

Or, perhaps they get squashed by someone who thinks they know better.

Think about your long-lost little kid dreams that make you smile.

Dig out your grade 2 school picture. GRIN.

Look that little kid version of you in the eye and ask...

What did your inner kid want you to be when you grew up?

Which ones still get your heart racing?

What steps could you take to get on that career path?

Let your inner little kid run the show.
He or she's been waiting a long time to get out and be heard!

"Adults are always asking little kids what they want to be when they grow up, cause they're looking for ideas."

Paula Poundstone, comic

Unexpected Mentor 12:

Embrace Your Gift Of Weirdness

Don't try to blend in.

Weirdness is a huge gift.

OK, start from the obvious with my hair. I can be spotted a mile away.

And, I own it. It's part of my weirdness. Hair that stands on end.

Even if someone can't remember my name, I become referenced as the woman with the crazy-sticky-uppy hair. And, yup, everyone knows it's me that's being referenced.

(You're likely thinking what *you'd* look like with hair that stands on end. GRIN.)

Weirdness also means being unique or finding ways to stand out.

I do the same with the marketing of my recruitment firm, TAG Recruitment.

There are well over 300 competing companies in Calgary alone.

To stand out takes unique marketing.

I certainly don't hand out pens or coffee mugs with my logo on them. HA. How boring is that?

Rather, I do fun, unexpected things.

I found a brand of vodka bearing the same name as my company – TAG Vodka.

What prospect client can resist an email from me with the subject line of "vodka?"

For fun, I have BBQ sauce branded with the TAG logo and a tag line of

"TAG Recruitment, recruiting Calgary's sauciest talent."

The sauce is delivered with our own signature Caesar cocktail recipe, of course using the TAG BBQ sauce and TAG vodka.

How fun is that?

Do the same with your career. Look for ways to NOT blend in.

Don't be afraid to stand out. Dive into your creativity and be recognized.

"Whatever makes you weird is probably your greatest asset."

Joss Whedon,
screenwriter, director, producer, comic book writer & composer

Mentor Moment

Your Turn!

What ideas simmer in your head about being a stand-out?

What weirdness have you been squashing?

What are your weird career assets?

Unexpected Mentor 13:

Your Silly Life

Life is full of hilarious moments and sometimes they are *embarrassing as hell.*

I use my silly life stuff as inspiration for my writing and speaking.

I started to write and publish a client/prospect newsletter after publishing my book. I'm sure the word "dull" popped into your mind when I said newsletter!

Let me assure you, my newsletter is the furthest thing from dull. I can pretty much guarantee the reader will laugh at least once.

I write about my Mom-Betty, my BFF James Bond, my cat Phoebe and simple silly life stories.

I've written about ***blowing the ass out of my dress*** while en route to a very chi-chi party this summer. And, I tied my dress debacle into "pressing the limits on staffing." It worked. HA. (This story still makes me laugh!)

I have to share. I used this photo from a race last summer in my newsletter.

I wrote about…

"things aren't always how they appear".

And, sometimes you need other people to point out a different perspective.

I posted this pre-race picture on Facebook. I couldn't figure out why it was getting so many "HAHA" comments.

Until, someone pointed it out…

Depending on what device the picture was being viewed on, most saw this image.

My hair became the ZZ Top beard on the guy standing behind me!
HILARIOUS!

My hair peaks were perfectly placed to align with his nose!

Sidebar – if anyone in Calgary knows who this dude is, pleaseeeeeee share this picture!

Throughout your career: **Things aren't always how they appear.**
AND, sometimes it takes friends/colleagues around you to point out
the OBVIOUS.

One more silly life story to share…

Good humour is always in fashion.

I bought a fitness tracker watch last winter. It appeals to my super competitive side.

Fast forward a few months.

I was having a stealth running week. Best ever.

Over the previous few weeks I'd noticed my arm was red under the rubber strap. So, I just moved it to a different spot on my arm. My arm was now itchy. So, I moved it to my right arm. Back onto the left arm the next day and so on. *(Taking it off didn't occur to me as I was tracking a phenomenal running week and didn't want to lose the results!)*

Well, I woke up the next morning with my arms and torso covered in red spots.

I dashed to my doctor. Yup – it was a fitness tracker band allergy.

She said,

"Just take Benadryl and you'll be fine.
But, be careful, because it can make you drowsy."

I chuckled and said,

"I'm due on stage in a few hours – and being *drowsy isn't a good characteristic of the keynote speaker*!"

Fast forward. I'm 20 minutes into my keynote.

I suddenly notice my upper lip feels numb.

My neck is hot. My ears are on fire.

All of these things are pretty noticeable when you've got super short hair.

I had no idea if I was breaking out in hives – or if my swelling lips were the size of a tractor tire or if my windpipe was going to start to close.

(Yes, this was going through my mind as I was delivering an hour-long keynote!)

I did make it through my keynote with only a numb lip. AND I had GREAT material to write about in a newsletter!

**Mentor
Moment**

Your Turn!

OK, back to you. You might be thinking,

How the heck can silly life stuff work in my career?

Think about all of the amazing lessons you've experienced that you can laugh about now.

I think it shows confidence and creativity. You probably didn't crumble like a cookie when silly life stuff happened and if you did – well - you learned from that too.

So, those serious doubts you may have about changing your career? *Your silly side actually gives you the guts to do it.*

(And, if you'd like to receive my fun and free newsletter, zip over to www.sheilamusgrove.com *to sign-up.)*

Unexpected Mentor 14:
Push The Impossible

This is me.

Balancing on a ball.

On one foot.

While wearing 4.5 inch stilettos.

Casually sipping coffee.

And reading the newspaper.

I'd say this was pushing the impossible.

My firm, TAG Recruitment has been recognized several times as one of Alberta's fastest growing companies. A magazine publisher had a great idea for a story.

Alberta had just come through a tough recession.

In a recession, no one is hiring. And, when you're in recruitment, hiring IS your sole business. The editor of the magazine thought up the idea of this photo to make it look like it was *"no big deal"* to get *through a recession.*

Back to the photo. When the magazine dropped, my phone rang like crazy.

People asked,

" Sheila, how the heck are you standing on that ball?"

I'd smile and simply say,

"glutes and abs, of course!"

I had loads of requests for the name of my trainer. GRIN.

But I had a secret....

I was actually standing on a box!

Which, given the heel height, was challenging enough!! The ball, including the clever dent were photoshopped in! There's no way in hell I could have stood on a ball but I certainly did the next best thing.

I love shortcuts like this.

Sometimes in your career there are clever shortcuts you need to take. And, often things aren't quite as hard as they might appear.

They help you push the seemingly impossible.

After being at college for a year, my confidence started to come in – and I got up the nerve to run for Student Government. Keep in mind, I was shy. Terrified to speak in public. And a bit nerdy.

Here was my first "seemingly impossible."

I was elected as Vice President and I then started on my university transfer program of studies.

A year later I ran for Students' Association President and won. I was elected to chair our student provincial organization that same year.

I got to have cool chats with the Minister of Advanced Education, college presidents and such at *the ripe old age of 21*.

I had 5 full-time staff.

I oversaw a newspaper publication and even a bar.

I had a 2 million-dollar budget.   All at the ripe age of 21.

Two years in Student Government was my career shortcut. I was handed a business to run. I drew on those two game-change experiences for many years.

I recall distinctly chatting with my GF the day I packed up my office at the Students' Association.

I said to her,

"When I grow up, I want a job just like this — to be the president of the Students' Association."

Years later, I realized what I was really saying was that I wanted to build and run a company.

Those 2 years were game changers. And, they fired up the hardwiring in my brain for running a business. They also showed me I could push what at first seemed impossible.

Mentor Moment

Your Turn!

Where can you push the *seemingly* impossible in your career? *Go there for a minute.*

What do you need to bridge the gap in skills/experience to get to that "seemingly impossible" level in your career?

What experiences can you go after to short-cut your career growth? *Think about volunteer experiences. Out of country work to gain valuable insights. A vertical move to get additional exposure.*

Unexpected Mentor 15:

Smart People Are Rocket Boosters

The students' association experience was shaped by one of my best friends – his name is James Bond and he is a dear friend to this day. He and I both served on our respective associations.

As soon as I met him, I thought, "Wow, smarty-pants".

He was smart. He was a "walking Google", well before Google existed. HA. He knew something about everything. I loved it. (I learned years later, he used to bring encyclopedias on family trips. He'd actually read them cover to cover. Who does that?? HA.)

And, all these years later, he is still one of the smartest people I know. I trust James completely and can always count on his wonderful outlook and feedback.

Smart can also come in the form of "good perspectives". You likely have people in your life who fall in that category too. They are the people who always have a slight twist on what is happening.

My pal Cyndi is that person for me. She sees things in a black and white way. No sugar coating. It's always the plain and simple. And, it almost always makes a ton of sense.

Both James and Cyndi are what I like to call "rocket booster" friends. A 5-minute conversation with them often feels like a ride on a rocket. It's quick. Sometimes you even get the stomach-lurch tingles. HA.

It's memorable. A rocket takes you where you're going FAST.

No time wasted. No dilly-dallying. Just to the point. And, crystal clear.

Rocket booster friends are a MUST.

Mentor Moment

Your Turn!

Who are the rocket boosters in your life?

Add more people like that to your life whenever you can.

Filter out the ones who drag you down. They are taking up space.

"I like constructive criticism from smart people."

Prince, musician

Unexpected Mentor 16:

The Word No

After I finished university, I was offered a full-time role with one of Canada's largest financial institutions. I did well and was very quickly put on their fast-track program.

And, for the one and only time in my career... *I was assigned a formal mentor.*

The first thing my mentor asked was, **"What level or job do you aspire to?"**

I confidently replied with,

"A VP level, of course."

He said without missing a beat,

"You'll need to move to Toronto to make that happen."

As attractive as the career path was – I loved Calgary and couldn't imagine moving away from my family and friends.

Knowing my career would be stalled by not relocating, I moved on quickly to a global staffing firm. My roles and responsibilities continued to expand. Still having my sights set on that VP title, I was invited to join the executive team!

...until I learned that it was based in Toronto.

While I might look like a big city girl, years later, I still couldn't imagine leaving Calgary.

I had to decline. I had a clever president; her name is Katherine King. She said,

"Well can you travel a lot?"

Absolutely. We had a deal. I joined the executive team and ran corporate sales for Canada.

Katherine was amazing. She was someone I looked up to and she was a mentor to me...whether she realized or not.

I remember one of her phrases to the executive team was,

"You'll always have a voice, but you might not always have a vote."

She was a natural in front of clients and tremendously engaging. She brought a fresh perspective to a worn-out culture.

She was a mentor who taught me so much.

Yes, sometimes mentors are leaders whom you simply *observe* and learn from.

(And they might not even know the impact they've had on you!)

She was tapped on the shoulder for her next move.   I was so sad to see her go!

The new interim president and I were like oil and water.

We. Did. Not. Mesh.

Soon after, I was busy with responding to a large bid. Taking a page from Mom and Dad's work ethic manual, I worked into the night over many nights to deliver a top-quality bid.

It was months in the making, and I closed my largest multi-million, multi-year deal.

That win was a career highlight. I loved my company and team.

But it was *still time to go* as my boss and I had opposing values.

It's always a good time to leave when your moral compass isn't aligning.

So I did.

Mentor Moment

Your Turn!

Where do you need to say NO in your career?

And, if your moral compass is reeling, like mine did, you definitely need to say a big NO.

Unexpected Mentor 17:

Career Flops Are
Your Friends

Even though I had been super successful in my previous job –
leaving it because of my former boss felt like a flop.

It really bugged me.

But deep down I knew I'd done the right thing.

I thought I'd just find another gig leading a sales team. That didn't
happen quite as I'd planned.

I spent the next 7 longggggggggg months searching for my next role.

And, out of the blue, I was approached by two industry colleagues to
do some consulting work. Months in, I was invited to join both
executive teams.

Are you ready?

CRAZY – I said no. To BOTH!

I had finally figured out what I was going to do. I would open a staffing firm!

I had wracked my brain on what kind of business I should open – wedding planner, event planner – who knew the answer was right in front of my nose?

With nowhere to go but up, I rented a single office in a really ugly business centre – it had blue carpet and pink chairs. It wasn't a place to invite clients.

Luck and timing are everything – within a month of opening, one of my former employees put me in touch with her new HR department and I secured an exclusive deal to recruit 40 sales professionals...within 6 weeks. OMG, I was a company of one! How the heck was I going to pull this one off???

By chance, I was at a networking event the next day and ran into an old client. She had just left her job and was freelancing. She was a god send to help me get this project and a few others off the ground. My little company was off and running.

My unexpected mentor of having a *career flop* business relationship actually led me to create my own company.

"You write a hit the same way you write a flop."

Allan Jay Lerner,
Academy & Tony award winner

**Mentor
Moment**

Your Turn!

Think about your career flops.
Some of them might make you chuckle. Some might make your stomach sink. Do it anyway.

Thinking about flops is a good exercise to see how they've shaped your career.

Have those flops put you on a better career path? *(If they haven't yet, know they will with time.)*

Unexpected Mentor 18:

Just One Damn Duck

Are you waiting to get your ducks in a row?

It's a BIG mistake.

I just started a company by building an IKEA desk and using a computer monitor as big as a fish tank. Zero clients and nowhere to go but up.

I want you to *just start* with whatever tools you have at this moment.

Wherever you are in your career:

Just start by selecting an unexpected mentor or two.

Just start with one step toward the career goal you have.

Just start with whatever tools you have.

The temptation to wait for perfection *before* action is huge.

It would have been easy for me to wait until…

…I had a nice office. (Not one with nasty pink chairs and blue carpet. GRIN.)

…A recruiter or two to help. (Rather than just ME.)

Clients with paying orders. (I didn't have one!)

…Candidates to present. (Nope, no candidates to work with either.)

…An unlimited amount of resources to attract candidates. (On-line job postings were fairly new in 2005 and they were damn expensive.)

I started small. My first recruitment ad was in a newspaper. It was what I could afford. And it worked! (A cut-out of the newspaper clip sits proudly on my desk as a reminder that I, "just started".)

"Start where you are. Use what you have. Do what you can."

Arthur Ashe,
professional tennis player & winner of three Grand Slam titles

The list of what would have been "nice to have" could have been paralyzing to the point of *nonaction*.

It's simply procrastination to wait until you have all of your ducks in a row.

I had to keep reminding myself to not focus on what I didn't have and rather *focus on action*.

What do I want you to do to change or better your career????

Don't worry about getting all of your ducks in a row.

Just start with one damn duck.

P.S. Yup. An Unexpected Mentor can even be a rubber duck.

Acknowledgements:

A small book made possible with some fabulously amazing people:

To my first unexpected mentors: Mom-Betty for teaching me how to write and Dad-Gene for teaching me how to be a great story teller. Love you.

To Kim Duke, editor-extraordinaire: Thank you for your enthusiasm in the seemingly endless rounds of edits. I so appreciate your laser sharp editing eye. We've had more than a few rounds of laughter throughout this project.

To Bro Ojrot: Your illustrations brought this book over-the-top. You "nailed" my crazy hair!!

To Tim Tamashiro, Cory Woron, The Style Guys – Jason and Aly: Thank you for allowing me to share your stories and images.

To kick-in-the-pants guy: The story of our conversation still makes me chuckle.

To James Bond & Cyndi Ruff: Thanks for being my rocket-booster friends for the last 30 years and counting.

To the keynote organizers & attendees: I'm grateful to have been able to stand on stages throughout the country to deliver the live version of this book. And, to all of the gals at the West Yellowhead conference who asked the question, *"Where's the book on this keynote?"*. Sometimes a bonk in the head is what's needed. GRIN.

To my team – Jake Hulse and Steven Trottier – Thank you for your dedication to TAG Recruitment. Our workplace is filled with humour and hard work. I'm grateful. (Thank you for staring at countless images of ducks with me. HA.) I appreciate your input!

To all of my dear friends, clients and supporters: You rock. I'm lucky to have you in my life.

To all of my unexpected mentors – Thank you for being part of my career and shaping experiences which became this book.

Other books by Sheila Musgrove:

"Hired! How To Get The
Zippy Gig. Insider Secrets
From A Top Recruiter."
2016. Available worldwide
on Amazon.

Volume Book Orders & Booking Sheila For A Speaking Engagement:

For more information on
volume discounts for bulk
book orders or to book
Sheila for a speaking
engagement:

sheila@hideseekfind.com or
visit: www.sheilamusgrove.com

Connect:

Instagram: @sheilamusgrove_author

Twitter: @SMusgrove_TAG

Facebook: @sheilamusgrove_author

LinkedIn: https://www.linkedin.com/in/sheilamusgrove/

Enroll in my blog: www.sheilamusgrove.com

Made in the USA
Monee, IL
07 May 2021